ANDREW LLOYD WEBBER™ PIANO SONGBOOK

5 EXPRESSIVE ARRANGEMENTS BY PHILLIP KEVEREN

Andrew Lloyd Webber™ is a trademark owned by Andrew Lloyd Webber.

ISBN 978-1-4950-9852-9

— PIANO LEVEL —
LATE INTERMEDIATE

HAL•LEONARD®
7777 W. BLUEMOUND RD. P.O. BOX 13819 MILWAUKEE, WI 53213

In Australia Contact:
Hal Leonard Australia Pty. Ltd.
4 Lenatara Court
Cheltenham, 3192 Victoria, Australia
Email: ausadmin@halleonard.com.au

Visit Hal Leonard Online at
www.halleonard.com

Visit Phillip at
www.phillipkeveren.com

PREFACE

Andrew Lloyd Webber is a modern master of the musical theatre. His awards, both as a composer and producer, include seven Tonys, seven Oliviers, a Golden Globe, and an Oscar. Knighted by Her Majesty Queen Elizabeth II in 1992, his music has won the hearts of music lovers the world over.

Arranging Andrew Lloyd Webber's music for the piano is a delight. His melodies are always appealing – immediately tuneful yet surprising as well. I hope you enjoy these settings!

Best regards,

Phillip Keveren

BIOGRAPHY

Phillip Keveren, a multi-talented keyboard artist and composer, has composed original works in a variety of genres from piano solo to symphonic orchestra. Mr. Keveren gives frequent concerts and workshops for teachers and their students in the United States, Canada, Europe, and Asia. Mr. Keveren holds a B.M. in composition from California State University Northridge and a M.M. in composition from the University of Southern California.

CONTENTS

ANGEL OF MUSIC
from THE PHANTOM OF THE OPERA

Music by ANDREW LLOYD WEBBER
Lyrics by CHARLES HART
Additional Lyrics by RICHARD STILGOE
Arranged by Phillip Keveren

ANOTHER SUITCASE IN ANOTHER HALL

from EVITA

Words by TIM RICE
Music by ANDREW LLOYD WEBBER
Arranged by Phillip Keveren

ANYTHING BUT LONELY

from ASPECTS OF LOVE

Music by ANDREW LLOYD WEBBER
Lyrics by DON BLACK and CHARLES HART
Arranged by Phillip Keveren

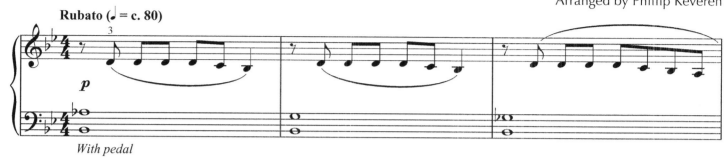

I DON'T KNOW HOW TO LOVE HIM

from JESUS CHRIST SUPERSTAR

Words by TIM RICE
Music by ANDREW LLOYD WEBBER
Arranged by Phillip Keveren

LEARN TO BE LONELY
from THE PHANTOM OF THE OPERA

Music by ANDREW LLOYD WEBBER
Lyrics by CHARLES HART
Arranged by Phillip Keveren

LOVE CHANGES EVERYTHING

from ASPECTS OF LOVE

Music by ANDREW LLOYD WEBBER
Lyrics by DON BLACK and CHARLES HART
Arranged by Phillip Keveren

LET US LOVE IN PEACE
from THE BEAUTIFUL GAME

Music by ANDREW LLOYD WEBBER
Lyrics by BEN ELTON
Arranged by Phillip Keveren

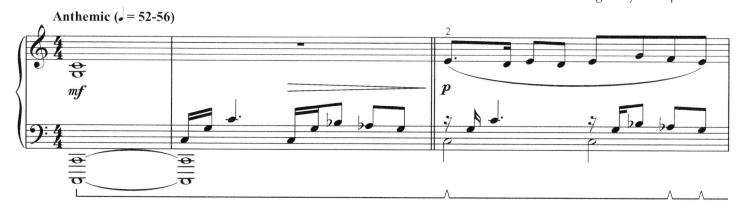

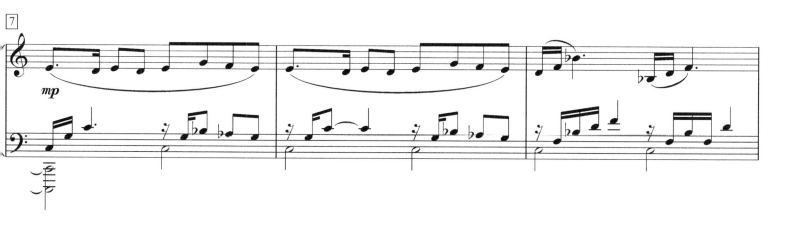

MACAVITY: THE MYSTERY CAT

from CATS

Music by ANDREW LLOYD WEBBER
Text by T.S. ELIOT
Arranged by Phillip Keveren

OLD DEUTERONOMY
from CATS

Music by ANDREW LLOYD WEBBER
Text by T.S. ELIOT
Arranged by Phillip Keveren

Slowly, with rubato (♩. = c. 84)

THE PERFECT YEAR
from SUNSET BOULEVARD

Music by ANDREW LLOYD WEBBER
Lyrics by DON BLACK and CHRISTOPHER HAMPTON
Arranged by Phillip Keveren

SUPERSTAR
from JESUS CHRIST SUPERSTAR

Words by TIM RICE
Music by ANDREW LLOYD WEBBER
Arranged by Phillip Keveren

THINK OF ME
from THE PHANTOM OF THE OPERA

Music by ANDREW LLOYD WEBBER
Lyrics by CHARLES HART
Additional Lyrics by RICHARD STILGOE
Arranged by Phillip Keveren

THE VAULTS OF HEAVEN

from WHISTLE DOWN THE WIND

Music by ANDREW LLOYD WEBBER
Lyrics by JIM STEINMAN
Arranged by Phillip Keveren

42

WISHING YOU WERE SOMEHOW HERE AGAIN

from THE PHANTOM OF THE OPERA

Music by ANDREW LLOYD WEBBER
Lyrics by CHARLES HART
Additional Lyrics by RICHARD STILGOE
Arranged by Phillip Keveren

YOU MUST LOVE ME
from the Cinergi Motion Picture EVITA

Words by TIM RICE
Music by ANDREW LLOYD WEBBER
Arranged by Phillip Keveren

THE PHILLIP KEVEREN SERIES

PIANO SOLO

ABBA FOR CLASSICAL PIANO
00156644...$14.99

ABOVE ALL
00311024...$11.95

AMERICANA
00311348...$10.95

BACH MEETS JAZZ
00198473...$14.99

THE BEATLES
00306412...$16.99

THE BEATLES FOR CLASSICAL PIANO
00312189...$14.99

BEST PIANO SOLOS
00312546...$14.99

BLESSINGS
00156601...$12.99

BLUES CLASSICS
00198656...$12.99

BROADWAY'S BEST
00310669...$14.99

A CELTIC CHRISTMAS
00310629...$12.99

THE CELTIC COLLECTION
00310549...$12.95

CHRISTMAS PRAISE HYMNS
00236669...$12.99

CHRISTMAS MEDLEYS
00311414...$12.99

CHRISTMAS AT THE MOVIES
00312190...$14.99

CHRISTMAS SONGS FOR CLASSICAL PIANO
00233788...$12.99

CHRISTMAS WORSHIP MEDLEYS
00311769...$12.99

CINEMA CLASSICS
00310607...$14.99

CLASSIC WEDDING SONGS
00311101...$10.95

CLASSICAL JAZZ
00311083...$12.95

COLDPLAY FOR CLASSICAL PIANO
00137779...$14.99

CONTEMPORARY WEDDING SONGS
00311103...$12.99

DISNEY SONGS FOR CLASSICAL PIANO
00311754...$16.99

FIDDLIN' AT THE PIANO
00315974...$12.99

THE FILM SCORE COLLECTION
00311811...$14.99

GOSPEL GREATS
00144351...$12.99

THE GREAT AMERICAN SONGBOOK
00183566...$12.99

THE GREAT MELODIES
00312084...$12.99

GREAT STANDARDS
00311157...$12.95

THE HYMN COLLECTION
00311071...$12.99

HYMN MEDLEYS
00311349...$12.99

HYMNS WITH A TOUCH OF JAZZ
00311249...$12.99

I COULD SING OF YOUR LOVE FOREVER
00310905...$12.95

JINGLE JAZZ
00310762...$14.99

BILLY JOEL FOR CLASSICAL PIANO
00175310...$14.99

ELTON JOHN FOR CLASSICAL PIANO
00126449...$14.99

LET FREEDOM RING!
00310839...$9.95

ANDREW LLOYD WEBBER
00313227...$15.99

MANCINI MAGIC
00313523...$12.99

MORE DISNEY SONGS FOR CLASSICAL PIANO
00312113...$15.99

THE MOST BEAUTIFUL SONGS FOR EASY CLASSICAL PIANO
00233740...$12.99

MOTOWN HITS
00311295...$12.95

PIAZZOLLA TANGOS
00306870...$14.99

POP STANDARDS FOR EASY CLASSICAL PIANO
00233739...$12.99

QUEEN FOR CLASSICAL PIANO
00156645...$14.99

RICHARD RODGERS CLASSICS
00310755...$12.95

SHOUT TO THE LORD!
00310699...$12.95

SONGS FROM CHILDHOOD FOR EASY CLASSICAL PIANO
00233688...$12.99

THE SOUND OF MUSIC
00119403...$14.99

SYMPHONIC HYMNS FOR PIANO
00224738...$14.99

TREASURED HYMNS FOR CLASSICAL PIANO
00312112...$14.99

THE TWELVE KEYS OF CHRISTMAS
00144926...$12.99

WORSHIP WITH A TOUCH OF JAZZ
00294036...$12.99

YULETIDE JAZZ
00311911...$17.99

EASY PIANO

AFRICAN-AMERICAN SPIRITUALS
00310610...$10.99

CATCHY SONGS FOR PIANO
00218387...$12.99

CELTIC DREAMS
00310973...$10.95

CHRISTMAS CAROLS FOR EASY CLASSICAL PIANO
00233686...$12.99

CHRISTMAS POPS
00311126...$14.99

CLASSIC POP/ROCK HITS
00311548...$12.95

A CLASSICAL CHRISTMAS
00310769...$10.95

CLASSICAL MOVIE THEMES
00310975...$10.99

CONTEMPORARY WORSHIP FAVORITES
00311805...$14.99

DISNEY SONGS FOR EASY CLASSICAL PIANO
00144352...$12.99

EARLY ROCK 'N' ROLL
00311093...$10.99

EASY WORSHIP MEDLEYS
00311997...$12.99

FOLKSONGS FOR EASY CLASSICAL PIANO
00160297...$12.99

GEORGE GERSHWIN CLASSICS
00110374...$12.99

GOSPEL TREASURES
00310805...$12.99

THE VINCE GUARALDI COLLECTION
00306821...$14.99

HYMNS FOR EASY CLASSICAL PIANO
00160294...$12.99

IMMORTAL HYMNS
00310798...$10.95

JAZZ STANDARDS
00311294...$12.99

LOVE SONGS
00310744...$10.95

RAGTIME CLASSICS
00311293...$10.95

SONGS OF INSPIRATION
00103258...$12.99

SWEET LAND OF LIBERTY
00310840...$10.99

TIMELESS PRAISE
00310712...$12.95

10,000 REASONS
00126450...$14.99

TV THEMES
00311086...$12.99

21 GREAT CLASSICS
00310717...$12.99

WEEKLY WORSHIP
00145342...$16.99

BIG-NOTE PIANO

CHILDREN'S FAVORITE MOVIE SONGS
00310838...$12.99

CHRISTMAS MUSIC
00311247...$10.95

CONTEMPORARY HITS
00310907...$12.99

HOW GREAT IS OUR GOD
00311402...$12.95

INTERNATIONAL FOLKSONGS
00311830...$12.99

JOY TO THE WORLD
00310888...$10.95

THE NUTCRACKER
00310908...$10.99

BEGINNING PIANO SOLOS

AWESOME GOD
00311202...$12.99

CHRISTIAN CHILDREN'S FAVORITES
00310837...$12.99

CHRISTMAS FAVORITES
00311246...$10.95

CHRISTMAS TRADITIONS
00311117...$10.99

EASY HYMNS
00311250...$12.99

EVERLASTING GOD
00102710...$10.99

KIDS' FAVORITES
00310822...$12.99

PIANO DUET

CLASSICAL THEME DUETS
00311350...$10.99

HYMN DUETS
00311544...$12.99

PRAISE & WORSHIP DUETS
00311203...$11.95

STAR WARS
00119405...$14.99

HAL•LEONARD®

Visit **www.halleonard.com**
for a complete series listing.

*Prices, contents, and availability
subject to change without notice.*

0917